JAN

THE
CONTEMPORARY
READER

VOLUME 3, NUMBER 2

Glencoe
McGraw-Hill

New York, New York   Columbus, Ohio   Chicago, Illinois   Peoria, Illinois   Woodland Hills, California

JAMESTOWN EDUCATION

Glencoe/McGraw-Hill

A Division of The **McGraw·Hill** Companies

Send all inquiries to:
Glencoe/McGraw-Hill
8787 Orion Place
Columbus, OH 43240-4027

ISBN: 0-07-827361-7

Printed in the United States of America

1 2 3 4 5 6 7 8 9 10 113 09 08 07 06 05 04 03

CONTENTS

Pronunciation Key

ă	mat	o͞o	food
ā	date	o͝o	look
â	bare	ŭ	drum
ä	father	yo͞o	cute
ĕ	wet	û	fur
ē	see	*th*	then
ĭ	tip	th	thin
ī	ice	hw	which
î	pierce	zh	usual
ŏ	hot	ə	alone
ō	no		open
ô	law		pencil
oi	boil		lemon
ou	loud		campus

*Why is mustard the spice of choice
all around the world?*

1 Ahhh! The great American picnic! Bring on the hot dogs, hamburgers, potato salad, and baked beans. One of the reasons why all these foods taste so great is the seasoning that we add to them—mustard. Americans love mustard and use it every day. Mustard has also been a favorite around the world for thousands of years. Mustard lovers on every continent are busy making changes to this super seasoning to keep everyone asking for even more mustard.

Mustard Goes Modern

2 You know what mustard looks and tastes like, right? Don't be so sure about that. It is true that

Mustard plants are not only beautiful, they also produce a seasoning that is popular the world over.

one type of mustard, a mild yellow spread, is the one that is most familiar to Americans. But every day, new mustards are being invented. In fact, folks at the Mount Horeb Mustard Museum outside of Madison, Wisconsin, have about 3,400 kinds of mustard on display. More are being added all the time.

3   Creative cooks are combining mustard with a wide variety of ingredients to make tasty new treats. For example, mustard has been combined with raspberries, with garlic, and with honey. If you're really adventurous, you might try chocolate fudge mustard or pineapple mustard. How about mustard flavored with lemon, peanuts, or black olives? The possibilities are endless.

4   Why is mustard so popular? For one thing, it contains almost no cholesterol.[1] In today's health-conscious world, that's a desirable quality, because people with high levels of cholesterol in their blood are more likely to suffer heart attacks. In addition, people are always willing to try new foods. They get tired of the same old meals and look for stronger, more exciting tastes. Mustard packs a big taste punch. It perks up almost any

---

[1] cholesterol: a substance connected with the formation of small, fatty deposits on the walls of the arteries. These deposits restrict the free flow of blood in the blood vessels.

Tourists at the Mount Horeb Mustard Museum examine a few of the 3,400 kinds of mustard on display.

bland taste, and it counteracts any greasy or overly sweet taste. Last, mustard mixed into food can stop some harmful bacteria[2] from growing. That means that foods containing mustard may stay fresh longer. Some companies that manufacture foods add mustard to increase their products' shelf life.

---

[2] bacteria: extremely tiny one-celled creatures

The basis of every prepared mustard, such as the distinctive Dijon mustard, is the seed of the mustard plant.

Where Mustard Comes From

5 Mustard is an herb that grows best in temperate climates. It thrives in the plains of western Canada. Mustard plants are grown on almost 700,000 acres in the western provinces.[3] It's a good thing that Canada can grow so many mustard plants. It takes a lot of plants to make even a small amount of mustard. The mustard seed is only 0.064 inches in diameter. To make one small jar of mustard takes 26,500 mustard seeds.

---

[3] province: a division of a country, similar to a state

6   After the mustard seeds are harvested, they are processed in one of two ways. They may be ground into a fine powder to be sold as dry mustard. Or they may be combined with other ingredients to make prepared mustard. Prepared mustard is the spread most of us buy in jars or squeeze bottles. It is made by combining ground mustard seeds with a liquid such as vinegar, wine, or water. Then various spices and other flavors are added. The spices that are added make a big difference in the final taste of the mustard.

Mustard Throughout History

7   Using mustard to jazz up food is not new. Some say that the practice dates back to about 3000 B.C., when mustard was first grown in India. In their writings, ancient Greeks mention enjoying the taste of spicy mustard. Ancient Romans mixed mustard with oils, vinegar, and honey. When the Romans went to France, they took mustard with them.

8   The French immediately took to mustard, adding it to their diets, sometimes to cover up the taste of meat that had become slightly rancid.[4] Mustard was so popular in France that many French cities competed to make the best

---

[4] rancid: having a bad smell or taste; rotten

mustard. The city whose mustard became most famous is Dijon. Dijon mustard is now known all over the world. The recipe is quite simple: Take black or brown mustard seeds. Grind them up and mix the powder with white wine or verjuice, the juice of grapes that are not quite ripe. No additives[5] or preservatives[6] are used. This recipe has been followed successfully for almost 400 years.

9   A taste for mustard has spread worldwide. Recipes from almost every continent call for this seasoning. Immigrants to America have brought their recipes with them. When classic yellow mustard was first introduced to the U.S. market in 1904, it tasted quite mild. That was the way most Americans liked it. But now anything goes as far as spicy heat is concerned. There is no single way that we Americans like our mustard, since our tastes are so varied. Each ethnic group that lives in America has introduced the rest of us to its kind of mustard, from mild to superhot.

---

[5] additive: a substance added, particularly to a food, to cause a change
[6] preservative: something that prevents a food from decaying or spoiling

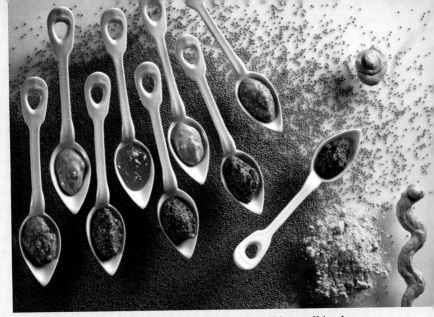

There is a mustard for every taste, from mild to call-in-the-firefighters hot.

Many Uses for Mustard

10 Everyone knows that mustard tastes good. But it also is good for you. Over the centuries, people have discovered some unusual uses for mustard.

11   Many people believe that mustard has the power to improve your health. They say that a dash of mustard in your food can help you digest your meals better. A taste of hot mustard can clear your sinuses[7] for hours. And for hundreds of years people used mustard plasters to increase blood flow to areas of the body that were inflamed.[8] To make a mustard plaster, they

---

[7] sinuses: air-filled spaces inside the bones in the skull that connect with the nose

[8] inflamed: having become hot, red, sore, swollen, or feverish

combined dry mustard and a little water to make
a thick paste. Then they smeared the paste on a
cloth and placed the cloth on the target area.
They had to be careful not to leave it on the skin
too long, because it could make the skin burn or
blister. Some people still believe in the healing
powers of mustard plasters.

12   Folk wisdom suggests using dry mustard to
stop the hiccups, to fertilize flowers, and to
protect your feet from frostbite on a cold winter
day. Do your hands smell like onions or fish?

Simply rub mustard on them, and your hands will smell better. (There's no word on whether they will just smell like mustard, but at least they won't smell like onions or fish.)

13   Mustard is truly a versatile[9] herb. However, for most people, mustard doesn't need to do anything but taste good. If you like mustard, be sure to celebrate National Mustard Day on the first Saturday in August. Have a picnic and put a jar of mustard in a place of honor. Then stand back as your guests rush for it. After all, a picnic wouldn't be a picnic without mustard. ◆

QUESTIONS

1. What are three reasons that mustard has become so popular?
2. What is the difference between dry mustard and prepared mustard?
3. Which country is relied upon for its mustard fields?
4. What is a mustard plaster, and how is it made?
5. Name three ways people have used mustard, other than as a food.

---

[9] versatile: having many uses

Fast-growing staghorn coral is a common sight along the Great Barrier Reef off the coast of Australia. It is one of about 350 different kinds of coral you can see there.

Exploring the
GREAT
BARRIER
REEF

*What is the Great Barrier Reef, and
what makes it remarkable?*

1   A sleek, silvery shape suddenly appears in the
blue-green water. Strong jaws and sharp teeth
snap shut on a plump parrotfish.[1] Just as swiftly
as it came, the barracuda[2] [băr ə kōō′də]
disappears into the deep waters on the seaward
side of the underwater ridge. On the more
protected landward side, life goes on as usual.
Hundreds of fish in all colors of the rainbow dart
in and out of the many hollows in the ridge.
Crabs scurry along the ocean floor. Creatures in
curious shapes and sizes move about in the clear
water. All are part of a fascinating world found in
one special place on Earth, the Great Barrier Reef
of Australia.

---

[1] parrotfish: any of a family of brightly colored tropical fish
[2] barracuda: any of a family of fierce tropical fishes

How the Reef Was Made

2 A reef is a wall-like structure made of sand, stones, or coral. Usually reefs form off the coast of an island and act as a breakwater, or barrier, between the land and the rough waters of the ocean. Most of a reef is underwater, but part of it is at or near the surface.

3 The Great Barrier Reef is not one solid coral reef. It is made up of about 2,900 separate reefs that stretch along the northeast coast of Australia for more than 1,250 miles. Coral reefs grow only under special conditions. The ocean must be shallow and warm and free from pollution. The area of the Pacific Ocean around the Great Barrier Reef is only 325 to 650 feet deep, and it is mostly in the tropical zone.

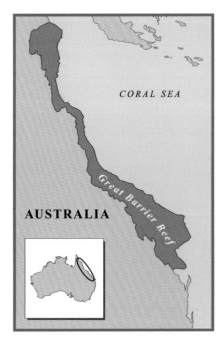

4 Scientists think that the Great Barrier Reef began forming about a half-million to a million years ago. It is hard to imagine, but the huge coral reef we see today started with the tiny animal

The coral polyp's skeleton is made of calcium carbonate. The skeleton acts as a home for the coral polyp and shields it from harm. When the coral polyp is threatened, it retreats inside its skeleton.

called the *coral polyp* [päl´ĭp]. Coral polyps can measure anywhere from less than .04 of an inch to more than an inch. An individual polyp looks like a small bag with an open mouth at one end. Around the mouth are tentacles,[3] which the polyp uses to gather its food. Most coral polyps live in groups called *colonies*. Each polyp in the colony builds a stony shell around its soft body. These shells are cemented together by a special kind of algae[4] [ăl´jē]. When a polyp dies, its hard skeleton remains. New polyps settle on top of the old

---

[3] tentacle: a long, thin feeler around the head or mouth of an animal

[4] algae: one-celled organisms that produce their own food but have no roots, stems, or leaves

Scuba-diving researchers examine the coral reef up close.

skeletons and add their skeletons to the pile when they die. Over hundreds of years, the coral wall grows larger and larger.

Exploring the Reef by Day

5 The best way to view the amazing sights of the Great Barrier Reef is by scuba diving.[5] As you swim along the reef, you can enjoy the colors of the upper, living section. The lower part of the reef, however, appears white. That section is

---

[5] scuba diving: swimming underwater with the aid of air tanks strapped to the back and connected to a mouthpiece by a hose

made of the skeletons of polyps that have died. In the many shapes formed by coral colonies, you recognize some of the 400 different kinds of coral found on the reef. *Staghorn* corals look like the antlers of a deer. They grow more quickly than most other types of coral and are very common in the Great Barrier Reef. Scattered here and there are *brain* corals. Their deep grooves and round shape make them look similar to a human brain, but they are much harder than our brains. Then you spot something that looks like the underside of a mushroom. It is the skeleton of a *mushroom* coral. Unlike the other kinds of coral, each mushroom coral is an individual polyp. One of these polyps can grow as large as five inches across.

6   As you swim through the water, a *sea anemone* [ə nĕmˊə nē] catches your eye. You first think it is another coral because it has a sack-like body and tentacles around its mouth. Don't get too close. The beautiful, flower-like tentacles contain a poison to stun small fish and other sea creatures, which the anemone then eats. It's clear that anemones find plenty of food on the Great Barrier Reef. Most sea anemones are just a few inches wide, but those on the reef grow up to three feet across. Perhaps you can spot the *clown fish* hiding in the tentacles of the sea anemone. The clown fish does not have to worry about the anemone's poison. This brightly

This clown fish appears to be swimming above a plant. But the "plant" is really a sea anemone, an animal with tentacles.

colored creature has a special coating on its skin that protects it. The anemone keeps the clown fish safe from predators. In return, the clown fish keeps the water moving so that sand cannot settle on the anemone.

7   The clown fish is not the only fish you see around the reef. The ocean is filled with schools of fish in every color of the rainbow. Their bright colors and wild stripes or spots dazzle your eyes. You watch them darting in and out of the reef searching for food. A large *grouper* slowly glides past you as it prowls through the coral canyons searching for prey. It steers clear of the *lionfish,* whose long spiny fins are filled with poison.

8   When you reach the shallow ocean floor, three brilliant blue *giant clams* catch your eye. You can see they are not like the clams you order at a seafood store. These can weigh more than 500 pounds and can measure four or five feet across.

9   Before you surface, you notice some *cowrie shells* and *cone shells* scattered among the reef rocks. Cowries and cones are mollusks, that is, animals with soft bodies that are usually covered with a hard shell. The Great Barrier Reef contains thousands of different kinds of mollusks.

Investigating the Reef at Night

10   As the sun begins to set, the ocean is filled with a flurry of activity. Vast schools of fish search for shelter within the reef. Their dazzling colors seem to fade as they blend in with their darker surroundings. The *triggerfish* disappears into a clump of seaweed. Its color and markings exactly match the pattern of the aquatic plants.

11   While the sea creatures that were active during the day sleep, others that had been hiding in the reef awaken. Shining your powerful flashlight on the ocean floor, you notice colorfully patterned *sea slugs* inching along. *Flatworms* emerge from their hiding places too. These are not like the worms you are used to seeing. These worms have rippled edges and are bright purple. Another creature creeps across your path. It is a *sea star.* These creatures are incorrectly called

Colorful coral is made up of living polyps. White coral is formed by polyps that have died over hundreds and thousands of years.

"starfish." A sea star is not a fish, however. Sea stars of the Great Barrier Reef usually have five "arms," but some sea stars can have as many as 50. You see another star-like creature, but this one looks more like a soft pillow. It is the *pincushion* sea star. Its five arms are not as separated as the arms of other sea stars.

12   Now is the best time to see the coral polyps. During the day their tentacles are closed within their hard shells. At night they open to catch the tiny plants and animals floating past them. Many of them look like flowers blooming in a dazzling array of colors. Yet corals are really animals, not

plants. Their color depends on which type of polyp they are and on the algae that live in and around the colony.

13   Both day and night, the Great Barrier Reef is filled with breathtaking sights. The reef provides the plants and animals with the food and protection they need to survive. In this special world, all of the inhabitants live in a delicate balance. ◆

QUESTIONS

1. Where is the Great Barrier Reef?
2. How is a coral reef formed?
3. What conditions are necessary for a coral reef to grow?
4. Name a sea creature that lives on the Great Barrier Reef, and describe one of its features.
5. How do the clown fish and the sea anemone help each other to survive?

Quilting requires a careful and steady hand.

THE ART OF QUILTING

*Why do we feel such affection
for the humble quilt?*

1 Imagine snuggling in your bed on a cold night
beneath a warm quilt. Now imagine that your
mother or grandmother made the quilt just for
you. It gives you the feeling of being loved,
doesn't it? That warm, cozy feeling is part of
what makes quilts so popular in the United
States and around the world. Now imagine that
the sun has come up and you are looking at the
quilt. It may dazzle you with its brilliant colors
and designs. Or it may soothe you with its
elegance.[1] The beauty of the quilt is another
reason that people have loved quilts for
hundreds of years.

---

[1] elegance: tasteful beauty

Quilting of Long Ago

2   Quilting began thousands of years ago. Records from ancient Egypt show people wore quilted clothing as long ago as 3000 B.C. The oldest existing quilt comes from Asia. It was found on the floor of a chief's tomb and was probably made at least 2,000 years ago.

3   Experts believe that Europeans learned about quilting from people in Palestine around the year A.D. 1095. The Europeans were impressed with the quilted jackets the Palestinian armies wore. The jackets were much lighter than the metal armor worn by the Europeans, and yet they were quite strong. Europeans took the idea of quilting home with them. Years later, when Europeans, Asians, and Africans came to the United States, they brought their skills in quilting along with them.

The American Quilt

4   In 19th-century America, quilting took a new turn. Instead of making quilted clothes, Americans began making quilted bedcovers. Men mostly ignored quilting, believing that it was women's work. Women were happy to take on the task. Quilting offered women a way to be creative and to help their families at the same time.

5   Early in our history, cloth was difficult to make and expensive to buy. Thrifty housewives who wanted to make simple quilted bedcovers reused fabric from worn-out clothes. By the middle of the 19th century, cloth was easier to obtain. Women could choose from a wide variety of cloth to make their quilts. The quilt became a work of art, in addition to being a bedcover.

6   Unlike some other forms of art, quilting requires almost no training. Anyone who can sew stitches can make a quilt. Women who had never been given a lesson in art worked on their quilts at night, after the mending was done. They chose patterns and colors that pleased them. In the process, they made outstanding works of art. Modern quilters still marvel at the beauty of these old quilts.

7   Although many women worked alone on their quilts, they also enjoyed sewing with others. In parties sometimes called quilting bees, women of the neighborhood would gather to create a single quilt. While sewing, they shared tips, techniques, and patterns. They also shared news of family joys and tragedies. The members of a quilting group became close friends for life. These quilters rarely sold any of the quilts they made. Instead, they gave them as gifts to their families and friends to celebrate milestone events, such as weddings and births.

Hawaiian women join in a modern quilting bee, chatting as they work together on a single appliqué quilt.

8   Quilting is as popular today as it was in the 1800s. Women, especially, see it as a great way to be creative. Like the women of the 1800s, they find they can make beautiful quilts without a great deal of training. And they continue to give quilts as gifts to the people they love.

Kinds of Quilts

9   What is a quilt and how is it made? The basic quilt has three layers. The cloth top is usually decorated with designs. The insulating[2] middle layer often is made of wool or cotton batting.[3] The bottom layer,

---

[2] insulating: preventing the loss of heat
[3] batting: layers or sheets of cloth

called the backing, is most often made of a plain fabric. The three layers are held together by long lines of fine stitching that go through all three layers. This stitching is called quilting.

10   Although the material used to make the middle layer determines how warm the quilt will be, the top attracts the most attention. The top gives the quilt its personality. There are three major kinds of quilt tops: whole cloth, appliqué [ăp lĭ kā´], and pieced.

11   A whole-cloth quilt top is a single piece of plain fabric. The beauty of the whole-cloth quilt comes from its complex quilting patterns. For example, a whole-cloth quilt with a white top and white quilting can have a quiet elegance. An appliqué quilt top begins with a large piece of plain cloth. Many small pieces of cloth are arranged into a design or a picture. Then the design or picture is sewn onto the large plain cloth. For a pieced quilt top, small pieces of cloth are sewn together in patterns. These small pieces form the entire top layer.

Traditional Patterns with Personal Touches

12   Quilters often follow traditional patterns to make their top layers. For example, one pattern that has been popular for more than a hundred years is called the log cabin. In a log cabin quilt, you

don't see a picture of a log cabin. Instead, you see a series of blocks made of narrow strips of cloth. At the center of each block is a tiny square. This square, which stands for the fireplace of a cabin, is often red. The strips, representing logs, are arranged around the central square. The quilter chooses the type of cloth, the width of the strips, and the colors for the pattern. Each choice makes that quilt a little different from any other.

13   This is one thing that makes quilts so amazing. Even though many quilters use the same pattern, each one can make a quilt that is unique. Each quilt expresses its maker's interests and personality.

Endless Variety

14 The various groups of people who live in the United States make quilts that match their tastes and culture. For example, the patterns of quilts made by African Americans often imitate West African textiles. The quilts are made of long strips of fabric sewn next to each other. These strip quilts often have repeating patterns, interrupted by additional eye-catching designs. Other quilts feature appliquéd panels that illustrate familiar African-American stories.

15   The people of Hawaii like to cover their quilts with graceful, curved decorations. Many Hawaiian quilts feature appliqués shaped like natural

Log cabins like the one in the distance were the inspiration for the traditional log cabin pattern seen in this brightly colored quilt.

objects such as flowers and fruits. Quilters attach the shapes to a plain cloth. Then they stitch again and again around the shapes, creating a kind of visual echo. Other Hawaiian quilts have a single symmetrical[4] [sĭ mĕ´trĭ kəl] shape in the

---

[4] symmetrical: the same on both sides of an imaginary line down the middle of the design or object

center. To make the shape, quilters fold a piece of fabric eight times and then cut through all the layers. This technique is similar to the way you would cut a paper snowflake. Then they appliqué the shape onto plain cloth.

16   An eight-sided, pieced star decorates most of the top of many Native American quilts. Native American quilters call this pattern the Morning Star. Venus, the morning star, moves across the sky throughout the year. To some Native Americans, this pattern has special meaning: It represents the path that the spirits of the dead use to come back to Earth.

Quilting Around the World

17   Quilting remains popular around the world. In Japan, especially, people have grown more interested in the art. It is common for quilters in Japan to use silk, not cotton as in the United States. The patterns or pictures on the quilt tops often are asymmetrical [ā´ sĭ mĕ´ trĭ kəl]. In other words, they are not the same on both sides of an imaginary line drawn down the middle of the quilt. Japanese quilters are also known for peaceful designs made of shades of blue that are quite close in color.

18   The art of quilting, begun long ago, has aged well. And it is moving confidently into the age

of the Internet. Like the quilting bees of the 19th century, online Web sites now provide ways for quilters to share patterns, tips, and techniques. Maybe, through their love of quilting, people will learn they are more alike than they are different. If so, quilts will have made the world a safer, warmer, and more beautiful place for us all. ◆

The ancient practice of quilting holds an attraction for modern artists and crafters.

QUESTIONS

1. Where was the oldest existing quilt found?
2. What was the purpose of quilting bees?
3. What are the three main types of quilts?
4. What is the significance of the Morning Star pattern for some Native Americans?
5. Why, do you think, do people enjoy making quilts?

Trumpeter Wynton Marsalis is a highly respected performer and teacher of jazz and classical music.

MARSALIS

MAKES

MUSIC

How has trumpeter Wynton Marsalis spread the good word about jazz?

1 Wynton Marsalis [wĭn´tən mär säl´əs] steps in front of the audience. He gives his fans a quick smile and picks up his trumpet. Then he launches into an upbeat tune. It's no wonder Wynton is happy. He is doing what he likes best—playing jazz. And he's swinging.

2   Inventor Thomas Edison once said, "Genius is one percent inspiration and 99 percent perspiration." Wynton would most likely agree with that statement. He knows that he was inspired by his family to be a musician. But he also knows that his success has come from plain old hard work.

A Family of Musicians

3   Wynton Marsalis was born in 1961 in a town just outside of New Orleans. His whole family was musical. Wynton's father was jazz pianist and music teacher Ellis Marsalis, Jr. Wynton's older brother, Branford, played the piano and the saxophone. Wynton's mother, Delores, hoped that all of her sons would become interested in music. With all this music around him, it's no wonder that Wynton became a musician. When he was 12 years old, he took up the trumpet. And once he took it up, he never put it down again.

4   When Wynton does anything, he really throws himself into it. That's how he approached learning to play the trumpet. Family members say he practiced morning, noon, and night. As a teenager, he found time to be an excellent student and to practice, practice, practice his music. Often, after everyone else had gone to bed, Wynton would go outside and practice under the stars.

5   Wynton's perseverance[1] and hard work were quickly rewarded. His family and his teachers were impressed with his talent and ability. When he was 18, he attended Juilliard [jo͞o´lē ärd], a famous music school in New York City. At Juilliard, he mainly studied classical music. Most

---

[1] perseverance: determination; drive

Wynton stands behind his brother Branford, as their father, Ellis, plays piano.

classical music comes from Europe, and much of it is quite old. Wynton understood that a complete musician should probably know all kinds of music. And he liked playing the classics. But he was beginning to understand that his heart belonged to jazz. After only about a year at Juilliard, Wynton got the chance to join a traveling jazz band. He knew that jazz music would be his future. So he quit school and went on the road with the Jazz Messengers.

United Nations Secretary-General Kofi Annan congratulates Wynton on being named a UN cultural ambassador.

Making a Career in Music

6 People soon began to notice that Wynton was no ordinary trumpet player. He played with a precision[2] beyond his years. His personal style was eye-catching too. He was cool, as only a jazzman can be, and was known for being a snappy dresser. A record company invited the young man to record on its label. Wynton recorded his first album, *Wynton Marsalis,* when he was only 19 years old. The album did well, but greater success was just around the corner.

---

[2] precision: exactness; accuracy; carefulness

7   The year 1983 was a successful one for Wynton. That's when he won two Grammy Awards.[3] This showed that he was talented at playing both jazz and classical music. Most people are good at one type of music or the other. Wynton was amazing at both. He received one Grammy for playing trumpet on his second jazz album. He got the other Grammy for his classical trumpet playing on another recording.

8   Success has followed Wynton ever since. He has triumphed as a performer and as a composer. In addition to recording several more jazz albums, Wynton has written music for dance companies. He was the first person to receive a Pulitzer Prize[4] for jazz. He won it in 1997 for *Blood on the Fields,* a piece that tells the story of slavery in music and words.

---

[3] Grammy Award: an award for special achievement in the U.S. recording industry

[4] Pulitzer Prize: an award that recognizes achievement in music, journalism, or literature

Spreading the Love of Jazz

9   Wynton is not only a great trumpet player, but he is also a caring teacher. Unlike most music teachers, he doesn't teach one student or one small class at a time. His students are all the young musicians he meets. His class is the world.

10   Wynton is known for his willingness to help music students. They often visit him backstage after concerts. Sometimes they want to hear his

Wynton Marsalis has the knack of making music understandable and fun for every audience.

opinion about their playing. Sometimes they just need a little motivation to keep on trying. Wynton is pleased to see these students care so much about music. So he takes a great deal of time to talk with them and give them feedback about their playing. His helpful words encourage them to continue with their music.

11   Wynton also teaches the world about jazz. Since 1987 he has been involved with the jazz program at Lincoln Center in New York City. He has served as the music director and as a trumpet player for the Lincoln Center Jazz Orchestra (LCJO). Under his direction, the orchestra has toured all over the world. The tours have gone to more than 250 cities in 30 countries on five continents. In concert, Wynton does more than just entertain his audience. He also teaches them about how to listen to and appreciate jazz. Wynton enjoys sharing his passion for jazz with others. He says, "Wherever the LCJO plays throughout the world, audiences have the same joyous reaction to the pulse of swing and the sweet sound of a singing horn."

12   Maybe you haven't been lucky enough to catch Wynton on tour. But you might have heard him on his radio series about jazz, called *Making the Music*. It highlighted the work of famous jazz musicians of the past. The series also looked at

different kinds of jazz, such as bebop[5] and fusion.[6] Or perhaps you caught his television show called *Marsalis on Music*. In it, he talked about jazz in ways that young people could easily understand.

---

[5] bebop: a kind of jazz developed from about 1945 to 1955 that uses quick, complex rhythms and chords

[6] fusion: a blend of jazz and rock music, made popular in the 1970s, that often features electric instruments

13   Recently, Wynton was featured in a PBS[7] series called *Jazz*. Listening to his lively explanations, viewers became excited about jazz themselves. In 2001 Wynton was named a United Nations Messenger of Peace. The title fits this man who has traveled around the world spreading his love for jazz.

14   Wynton Marsalis has combined precision and passion in his career. Because of him, jazz musicians of the past have not been forgotten. And perhaps, because of him, future jazz musicians will be encouraged to keep practicing and to keep swinging. ◆

Q UESTIONS

1. Besides Wynton, which members of the Marsalis family are musicians?
2. Why did Wynton join the Jazz Messengers?
3. Why was 1983 a special year for Wynton?
4. How does Wynton show that he cares about young musicians?
5. How does Wynton teach the world about jazz?

---

[7] PBS: Public Broadcasting System

Imagine finding a wall painting like this as you explore a cave. This drawing of a running bison may be 31,000 years old.

Hidden in the DARK

How did two discoveries change our view of prehistoric cave societies?

1 One afternoon, four young men, armed with a knife, a small oil lamp, and a rope, made an amazing discovery. Earlier, one of the boys had noticed a deep hole in the ground next to a newly fallen tree. He asked his friends if they wanted to go exploring with him. He said they might find buried treasure. The other boys jumped at the chance. The year was 1940, and the place was Lascaux [lăs kō´], in southern France.

The Discovery at Lascaux

2 When the boys reached the hole, they cleared stones away from its entrance. Then they lowered themselves into the dark. They found that the hole was a passageway to a large cave.

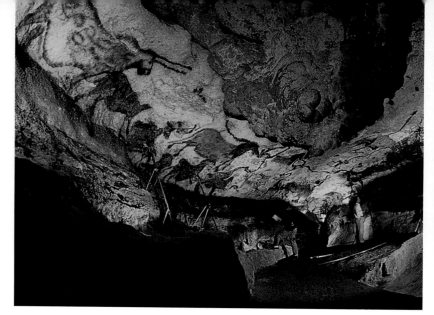

This 17,000-year-old painting was found in a section of Lascaux known as the Hall of the Bulls.

When they played the dim light of their lamp on the cave walls, they were amazed to see colorful paintings. The paintings showed red cows, yellow horses, and black bulls and stags[1] racing across the walls and ceiling of the cave. The young men had indeed found a treasure, even though it was not the kind they had expected.

3   Excited by their discovery, they returned the next day and searched farther into what turned out to be a series of caves. All around them were mysterious paintings. The boys couldn't keep this news to themselves and soon told their families and friends. When other villagers heard about the

---

[1] stag: an adult male deer

paintings, they hurried to see the site. Soon
scientists and archaeologists followed.

What They Found

4 What was the excitement about? The teenagers
had stumbled onto one of the major finds of the
20th century. Everyone who saw the paintings on
the walls could tell that they were very old.
(Scientists have since determined that the
paintings were made about 17,000 years ago.)
And what beautiful and powerful paintings they
were! In one of the biggest caves, the Hall of the
Bulls, the ancient artists had painted a giant
mural.[2] It showed large, life-like bulls surrounded
by running horses and graceful horned stags. In
other parts of the cave system, they had painted
imaginary creatures, such as a two-horned animal
with four legs and oval markings on its body.
Most pictures were engraved[3] into the rock and
then painted with yellows, reds, oranges, browns,
and grays. The colors were as bright as if they
had been painted yesterday.

5 Modern artists were amazed at the fine quality
of the paintings. They could tell that the artists
had painted quickly. The strokes were confident

---

[2] mural: a large painting usually used to decorate a wall
or ceiling

[3] engraved: formed by cutting into material such as stone or
hard wood

and expert. The paint was not simple charcoal picked up from an old fire pit. Instead, it had been carefully prepared. For example, to make black paint, the artists had to heat bone to about 400 degrees Celsius and then grind it into a powder. They had to add powdered minerals to create paints of other colors.

6   Modern artists also studied the techniques used in the paintings. The cave artists used techniques that most experts had thought were

Techniques used by ancient artists almost match those of more modern artists. Because of its similarity to Chinese art, this Lascaux painting is called "Chinese Horse."

more recent inventions. They used perspective, a way of making scenes look three dimensional. They used shading to create a life-like effect. In fact, their techniques were so good that experts believe that these artists had no job other than to create beautiful things. Even though daily life was a struggle, the group valued art highly enough that some members gave it their total attention. Such an idea is at odds with our usual image of a near-savage cave society.

7   In addition to the pictures of horses, bulls, and deer, the artists had painted mysterious symbols. Dots, arrows, lines, and squares cover some walls. What did these symbols mean to the people who made them? No one knows.

Sharing with the World

8 People all over the world were eager to see what their ancestors had created. Starting in 1948, when the cave was opened to tourists, crowds visited at the rate of about 600 people per day. For years, body heat from these crowds raised the temperature in the caves. Slowly, humidity in the cave's air increased. A film of water formed on the paintings. Paint started to flake off, and green mold began to grow on the walls. Paintings that had remained perfect for 17,000 years were being destroyed.

9   Concerned officials installed ventilation[4] systems in 1958 to allow the moist air to escape. But the number of visitors kept growing, and so did the mold. In 1963, the cave finally had to be closed to the public. Luckily, a careful cleaning of the walls removed most of the mold. Even so, officials decided never to open Lascaux to the public again. Today, only 20 carefully chosen people per week may enter the cave. To keep the level of the moisture low, visitors must leave after only 35 minutes.

10   The French people know that the cave at Lascaux belongs to the world. That's why they have made a copy that anyone can visit. Lascaux II is an exact replica[5] of the cave, made from molded concrete. To create Lascaux II, photographers took pictures of the paintings in the real cave. Then an artist copied them onto the walls and ceiling of the replica. Since Lascaux II opened in 1983, about 300,000 tourists have visited it every year.

Chauvet Cave

11 As amazing as the Lascaux cave is, another cave recently found in the south of France may turn out to be even more wonderful. It was discovered

---

[4] ventilation: a way to allow fresh air to flow through a place

[5] replica: a copy of an original

The Lascaux and Chauvet caves are in an area of southeast France with many natural caverns.

in 1994 by three cave explorers. One of the explorers, Jean-Marie Chauvet [shō vā´], is also an expert in rock art. When he entered the cave with his friends and saw the fantastic paintings on the walls, he knew at once that this cave was precious. Luckily, Chauvet was familiar with the problems at Lascaux. Very soon after finding the cave, he laid plastic sheeting on the cave floor. He wanted to make sure visitors' shoes didn't destroy something that could never be replaced.

12   How is the Chauvet Cave different from Lascaux? For starters, the Chauvet paintings, which are similar to Lascaux's, are much older. In fact, they are an incredible 31,000 years old!

Although experts had believed that the Lascaux artists knew much more about painting than those who had gone before, Chauvet made them change their minds. The painting techniques at Chauvet are similar to the ones at Lascaux. Clearly, ancient artists had known these techniques 14,000 years before the artwork in Lascaux was begun.

13   The animals on the walls of each cave also are different. At Lascaux, artists painted the gentle animals that ancient people hunted, such as cows and deer. At Chauvet, the artists filled the walls with paintings of dangerous animals. They pictured rhinos, bears, and a panther. And only Chauvet is littered with bones—it holds the bones of about 40 bears. Did the cave people kill or worship the bears there? Was the cave used as a kind of art gallery or sacred gathering place? A place of initiation[6] or trial? A place for priests of the tribe to work their magic? Again, no one knows, but experts are working hard to find the answers.

14   French officials learned their lesson well at Lascaux. They have set strict rules about who can enter the Chauvet cave and how visitors must dress. The few people allowed into the cave must wear special suits and shoes. The goal is to

---

[6] initiation: a ceremony during which a person becomes a member of a group, such as a club

have as few exchanges between people and the cave environment as possible. Officials hope to keep the air that touches the paintings the same as it has been for more than 30,000 years. Just as Lascaux was copied to make Lascaux II, a replica of the Chauvet cave is in the works. It is scheduled to open in 2003.

15   Hidden in the dark of these caves, we come face to face with the works of those who came before us. In some caves, searchers have found handprints of the artists who painted there so many years ago. Perhaps the artists left the prints as their signature. Using these handprints, we can guess how those people looked. Even more important, by studying their paintings, we can begin to understand how they thought and felt. ◆

Q UESTIONS

1. Who discovered the Lascaux cave? Who discovered the Chauvet cave?

2. Why are artists impressed with the paintings in these caves?

3. Which animals are pictured in the Lascaux cave? In the Chauvet cave?

4. What are some ways that ancient people may have used the caves?

5. Why did French officials create Lascaux II?

ROYALTY
ON THE WING

*Where and why does this
beautiful butterfly migrate?*

1   Imagine an early fall day. You look up and see
the stirring sight of a flock of birds heading
southward. But look again. Are those winged
figures really birds? They could be monarch
butterflies, migrating to warm winter homes.

Life Stages

2   When you see a monarch butterfly up close, you
certainly know that it isn't a bird. The adult
monarch butterfly is a distinctive insect with
bright orange-and-black wings. It is quite large—
that is, for a butterfly. Its wingspan[1] may reach a
respectable four inches.

---

[1] wingspan: the distance from the tip of one wing to the
tip of the other

**Hundreds of monarch butterflies cling to a tree branch in
Natural Bridges State Park, California. During the winter,
monarchs seek warmth in California and Mexico.**

3   Before it can begin its flight south, the monarch must go through four life stages: egg, larva, pupa [pyōō´pə], and adult. Monarchs begin life as tiny eggs. Each monarch has about 400 brothers and sisters. All the eggs are laid at the same time on milkweed plants. Milkweed is very important to monarchs. Their first meal is milkweed leaves, and milkweed is their only food until they become adults.

4   After the eggs hatch, monarchs begin their second stage of life. They have become larvae [lär´vē], or caterpillars. Monarch caterpillars are

This hungry monarch caterpillar has just emerged from its egg and is ready for its first meal of milkweed leaves.

champion eaters. Starting on their first day of life, they eat almost constantly. They stop only briefly to rest. Eating all that food helps them grow quickly. As they grow, the caterpillars molt [mōlt], or shed their skins. They grow so quickly that they must shed their outgrown skin every three or four days. After four or five molts, they reach their full size of about two inches. Then they weigh about 2,700 times what they weighed when they hatched. If you weighed eight pounds at birth, and you gained weight at the same rate as a monarch caterpillar, within about 16 days you would weigh almost 11 tons!

5   At this point, the monarch enters its third stage, called the pupa stage. The caterpillar instinctively looks for a place where it will be safe. When it finds the right spot—the underside of a twig, for example—it spins a wad of silk from a gland[2] near its mouth. It attaches the silk wad to the twig and grasps the silk wad with its hind legs. Then it hangs upside-down in the shape of a J for between 12 and 19 hours. Finally, the caterpillar twists and shakes and sheds its skin for the last time.

6   The new skin that is revealed looks like a soft, light green blanket covering the caterpillar. Once the skin dries and it hardens, its color changes to a darker jade green. It has golden dots or a golden rim around the top. The caterpillar is now

---

[2] gland: a bodily organ or group of cells that produces a substance

a chrysalis [krĭs´ə lĭs]. The chrysalis is sometimes called a pupa. As time passes, amazing changes occur within the chrysalis. The caterpillar undergoes a change of form, or metamorphosis [mĕt´ə môr´fə sĭs], from caterpillar to butterfly.

7   After about two weeks, the butterfly can be seen within the now-clear outer skin. Finally—

After its amazing metamorphosis, a monarch butterfly emerges from the dried skin of its chrysalis stage.

usually on a warm, sunny day—the adult butterfly pushes out, wrinkled and wet. Still clinging to the clear case that used to be its home, it pumps fluid into its wings to make them spread out. After opening and closing its wings for about two hours to dry them off and harden them, the butterfly flies away. It is searching for its first meal in weeks. Now its diet is no longer milkweed leaves. Instead, it will suck nectar[3] from inside flowers and drink water from streams and puddles.

---

[3] nectar: a sweet liquid produced by a plant

The Monarch Butterfly Migration

8 Monarch butterflies emerge at two times during the year. Those that emerge in spring and early summer live for only about a month. Monarchs that emerge in the fall, however, live several months and have much more exciting lives: These migrant monarchs are the ones that fly in huge groups to faraway places with warmer climates.

9 On their fall flight, monarchs reach impressive speeds of 10, 20, or even 30 miles per hour. Along the way, they alight on plants for quick sips of nectar and then continue. At night they roost on trees and bushes, since they cannot fly in temperatures below 55 degrees Fahrenheit. And where are they headed? Experts tell us that monarchs from east of the Rocky Mountains fly to forests high in the mountains of central Mexico. Monarchs from west of the Rocky Mountains travel to groves of trees along the California coast. The western monarchs may fly only a few hundred miles. However, the eastern monarchs may fly close to two thousand miles from southern Canada to Mexico.

10 During these long flights, monarchs are always in danger of being eaten by other animals, especially birds. But monarchs rely on an interesting form of protection. The milkweed

plants that the monarchs eat as caterpillars contain a poisonous substance. A hungry bird may try to eat a monarch butterfly once. When it finds out how bad monarchs taste, however, it will never eat one again. Birds learn to recognize the bright color of the monarchs and look elsewhere for a light snack.

Lazy Days of Winter

11   A huge crowd of fellow monarchs awaits the travelers. As many as five million monarchs cluster in California, and about a billion gather in Mexico! The trees in both of these areas may become completely blanketed with monarch butterflies. Scientists say that a single tree can hold 15,000 to 20,000 butterflies. And the next year, the descendants[4] of these butterflies will most likely stop at the exact same trees that were covered the year before.

12   The butterflies spend the winter in the warm areas. Since they have no internal[5] way to heat themselves, they depend on the sun for warmth. When they are hot, they cool off by flying. Finally, in February or March after a long, lazy winter, the monarchs prepare to make their return trip.

---

[4] descendants: generations that follow
[5] internal: inside; built-in

The monarch butterfly's beautiful orange color serves to teach predators that their intended meal might be toxic.

13   On warm days in these months, millions of monarchs take to the sky at the same time. On the journey, the females lay their eggs on milkweed plants along the way and die soon after. Their offspring[6] continue the migration northward, and the cycle starts again.

Migration Mysteries

14   Why do monarch butterflies migrate? The answer is . . . nobody knows. Monarchs cannot survive in temperatures much below freezing, so flying

---

[6] offspring: children

Who would suspect that this delicate butterfly could fly 2,000 miles in its winter migration?

south to warmer temperatures makes sense. Still, nobody knows how the migration to Mexico and California started.

15   How do monarchs know where to go? Again the answer is . . . nobody knows. Scientists, however, have many theories. Some think that the butterflies use the sun as a compass. Others believe they use Earth's magnetism[7] to guide them. At this point, it is an unsolved mystery.

The Future of Monarch Migrations

16   Some scientists believe that the monarch migrations may not last much longer. More and more people are moving into the areas where monarchs spend their winters. In California, houses have been built on some of these sites.

---

[7] magnetism: a basic force that a material, such as iron, has for attracting another material

The butterflies have been forced into smaller and smaller spaces. In Mexico, forests where monarchs like to roost have been cut down. In addition, herbicides[8] are killing the milkweed plants that monarchs depend on, both at their summer homes and along their migration routes.

17   Monarch lovers are working to save the groves of trees and the milkweed plants. Will they succeed? If not, we may not have many more chances to see this spectacular sight—thousands of orange-and-black monarch butterflies sweeping across the blue fall sky. ◆

QUESTIONS

1. What colors can be seen on a monarch butterfly's wings?
2. Name the four life stages of the monarch butterfly.
3. Where do the butterflies from east of the Rocky Mountains spend the winter?
4. What protects the monarch from birds?
5. What recent changes have affected the areas where monarch butterflies spend their winters?

---

[8] herbicide: a chemical that destroys plants or stops their growth

Clara Barton

❧ *and the* ❧

AMERICAN RED CROSS

How did the American Red Cross begin?

1   A tornado rips through a town. It leaves wrecked homes and downed trees in its path. A muddy river rushes out of its banks, flooding towns and farms. An apartment fire leaves its victims without food or shelter. When such disasters occur, we often spot a familiar sign at the scene. We see a red cross on a white background, the symbol of the American Red Cross.

2   We all know that Red Cross volunteers help people in times of trouble. But few people are aware of how the organization began. It was started through the efforts of a single woman with a strong will. Her name was Clara Barton.

In this 1902 photo, Clara Barton proudly wears the symbol of the organization she brought to the United States, the Red Cross.

The Shy and Quiet One

3   To those who knew Clara Barton as a child, it did not seem possible that one day she would be talking to presidents and members of Congress. Clara was born on December 25, 1821, in North Oxford, Massachusetts. She was much younger than her two brothers and two sisters. She was very bright but extremely shy and quiet. When she was 11 years old, one of her brothers fell and injured himself badly. she stopped her schooling for a while in order to take care of him. This experience marked the beginning of her love for nursing. That love would last throughout her life.

4   After Clara returned to school, she decided to become a teacher. She hoped that being a teacher would help her overcome her shyness. At the age of 17, she completed her studies and began her teaching career. As a teacher, she not only overcame her shyness, but she also learned valuable lessons in organizing and managing.

Clara and the Civil War

5   After many years of teaching, Barton decided to make some changes in her life. She quit teaching and went to work at a new job. She became the first female clerk at the U.S. Patent Office in Washington, D.C. Although Clara was interested in her work, she still felt a need to help others.

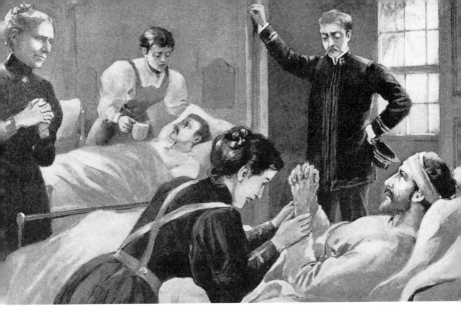

Ignoring danger and hardships, Clara Barton nursed wounded soldiers at battlefront hospitals during the Civil War.

6   A few years after the start of her job at the Patent Office, the Civil War began. One day Clara ran into a group of soldiers from her home state of Massachusetts. They had lost all their belongings during a battle. Clara seized the long-awaited chance to do something useful for others. Immediately, she began collecting supplies and cooking soup for the soldiers.

7   As the war continued, Clara grew more and more disturbed by reports of how wounded soldiers were being treated. She heard, for example, that they often had no bandages or food. She felt that she could no longer ignore their needs and maintain her quiet life. So she quit her job in order to spend more time helping needy soldiers. She wrote letters to friends and

put an ad in the local newspaper, asking for supplies. It seemed that many people welcomed the chance to help. They sent so many items that Barton had to open a warehouse to store them. In 1862 she received permission to take the supplies directly to the battlefront.

8   For two years Clara faced the dangers of war as she delivered supplies wherever they were needed. She didn't simply make her deliveries and then retreat to a safe city, however. Instead, she spent a great deal of time at the camps. She

Whether the crisis is a war, a fire, a storm, or some other disaster, the Red Cross is there to help. In this photo, victims of a flood in Austin, Texas, await aid.

nursed the wounded and cleaned the makeshift[1] hospital rooms. She was so close to the fighting that a bullet once passed through her sleeve and struck the man she was tending. The man was killed, but Clara escaped with only a hole in her dress. She grew more determined. It would take more than that to stop Clara Barton from helping!

9   After the Civil War, Barton decided to continue her work. She knew that many soldiers were still missing. She felt sorry for their loved ones, who longed to know what had happened to them. She asked for and was given the job of searching for missing soldiers.

10   Before long, all of the hardships that Clara had gone through made her ill. She became completely exhausted. Her doctor advised her to take a long rest. So she decided to go to Switzerland.

A New Goal for Clara

11   Even though Clara meant to rest, she found that soldiers in Europe needed her too. Soon after she got there, war broke out between Germany and France. With her battlefield experience, Barton knew she could be of use. She worked with a group called the International Red Cross. She delivered supplies to soldiers and prisoners on both sides of the conflict.

---

[1] makeshift: temporary; used for a while in place of the real thing

12   While in Europe, Clara learned about an agreement that many European countries had signed, called the Geneva Convention. This agreement provided for the delivery of impartial[2] aid to the wounded, sick, and homeless during wartime. Because of the Geneva Convention, the International Red Cross was allowed to travel safely through battle lines. Red Cross volunteers were considered neutral. That is, they would not take sides in a battle. Clara worked tirelessly with the International Red Cross for almost a year. For her service, the German emperor awarded her the Iron Cross of Merit.

13   In 1873 Clara returned home. She was determined to establish the Red Cross in the United States. She knew that she would have to overcome a huge obstacle in order to achieve her goal. She would have to convince the U.S. Congress and the president that they should sign the Geneva Convention. Only after they agreed could she begin a U.S. chapter of the Red Cross.

14   Clara began the task with her usual energy and drive. She wrote letters to members of Congress urging their support. She gave speeches explaining the Geneva Convention and why it would be good for the United States. She visited members of Congress and met with the

---

[2] impartial: not taking sides

After a tornado, a Red Cross worker aids a woman at the remains of her home.

president's advisors. It seemed, however, that almost no one agreed with her. The president and Congress thought that if they signed, foreign countries would be more likely to meddle in U.S. affairs. The United States wanted to isolate[3] itself from other countries as much as possible. Besides, Congress said, there already were groups to help soldiers. In their opinion, the Red Cross was not needed.

15   Clara was discouraged, but she refused to give up her plan. When James Garfield was elected president four years later, Clara tried again to persuade the United States to sign the Geneva

---

[3] isolate: to set apart

Convention. President Garfield was willing to listen. Barton was so encouraged that she and her supporters officially founded the American Red Cross Society on May 21, 1881. That was before the agreement was finally signed.

The American Red Cross

16 Barton became the first president of the new organization. She immediately began organizing chapters.[4] The first chapter was founded in Dansville, New York. Later, volunteers began chapters in other New York cities. The chapters were put to the test very quickly when a huge forest fire broke out in northern Michigan. The American Red Cross sent money and supplies to its victims.

17 Realizing that the group needed to be prepared at all times, Clara began raising more money and supplies. She wanted to be ready for the next disaster. During the 23 years that Clara served as president, there were floods, earthquakes, fires, and even a war. Sometimes it was a struggle to get enough supplies, but the American Red Cross was there in every disaster.

18 Red Cross founders had begun the organization to assist soldiers in time of war. Clara believed, however, that the victims of any disaster needed help, whether in war or in peace.

---

[4] chapter: a local branch of a group or organization

As a delegate[5] to the Third International Conference of the Red Cross, Barton spoke to the group about the peacetime work of her chapters. As a result, the other delegates agreed that the Red Cross should aid anyone in need. They called this new rule the American Amendment[6] in honor of Clara.

19   Clara Barton set high goals for herself and achieved them through hard work. She helped people in need and founded a group that continues her work to this day. One person made a big difference in our world. What an example she set for us!

QUESTIONS

1. How did becoming a teacher help Clara?
2. How did Clara help soldiers during the Civil War?
3. What steps did Clara take to persuade the United States to accept the Geneva Convention?
4. When was the American Red Cross founded?
5. What is the American Amendment of the International Red Cross?

---

[5] delegate: a representative sent to a meeting or conference
[6] amendment: a change or addition, especially to an official document, such as a bill or a law

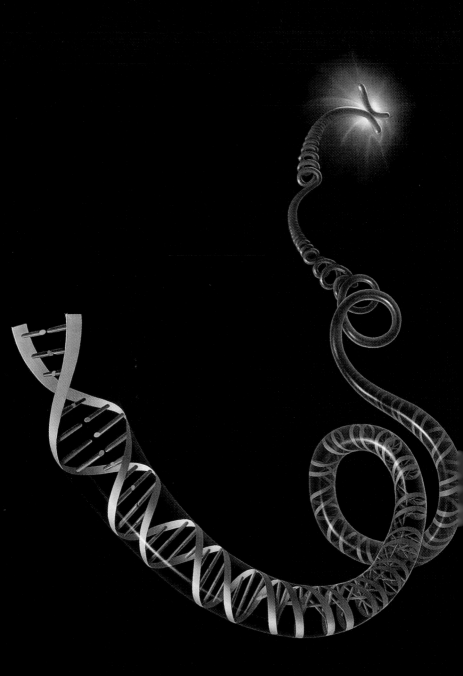

DNA looks like a long, coiling ladder. Genes are sections of the ladder.

WORKING WITH GENES

Why can't a cornstalk grow apples? Or can it?

1   What makes babies look like their parents? Why does a cat have kittens, and not puppies? When you plant a flower seed, why does a flower sprout, and not a radish?

2   Scientists think they have some answers to these questions, but their answers have raised even more questions. Our knowledge about how living things grow gives us power to change those things. But will we change them for the better? Work being done with genes [jēnz] today will affect all of us.

Mother Nature's Genes

3   What is a gene? To answer that, we first look at a cell. A cell is one of the small units that make up each living thing. In a human body, there are more than 75 trillion of them—skin cells, bone

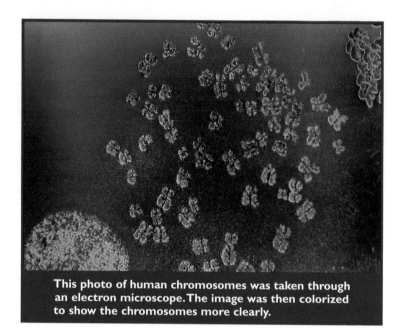

This photo of human chromosomes was taken through an electron microscope. The image was then colorized to show the chromosomes more clearly.

cells, muscle cells, brain cells, and others. Each cell contains a nucleus [noō´ klē əs], the "brains" of the cell. Inside the nucleus are rod-like structures forming an X. These structures are called *chromosomes* [krō´ mə sōmz´]. The number of chromosomes in a cell depends on the kind of plant or animal the cell comes from, but they always come in pairs. For example, a fruit fly has only 8 chromosomes, or 4 pairs. A human has 46 chromosomes, or 23 pairs.

4   A chromosome is made up of DNA[1] and the proteins attached to it. DNA is formed of long

---

[1] DNA: an abbreviation for deoxyribonucleic acid, found in the nucleus of cells

strands of thread-like material. If you could unravel all the DNA threads in all the cells of your body and lay the threads end to end, they would reach from Earth to the Moon about 6,000 times!

5   The DNA itself is shaped like a ladder whose sides coil around and around. Each rung on the ladder is made up of two compounds,[2] one attached to each side. Only four compounds are ever used to make the rungs of the ladder. They are often referred to by their initials: A, T, C, and G. A combines only with T, and C combines only with G. There are only four possible combinations: A-T, T-A, C-G, and G-C. But they can be arranged in a wide variety of patterns. This

_____

[2] compound: a substance containing two or more elements that have been chemically combined

means that even though all plants and animals have DNA in their cells, the DNA code is different for each organism.[3] Corn DNA tells the corn plant to grow ears of corn. Cat DNA tells the babies to grow into kittens. And human DNA determines our height, our skin and eye color, and many other things about our bodies and how they run.

6   Surprisingly, not all of the DNA in the chromosome actually does anything—at least, that we know of. Some of it just seems to be there to connect the important sections. Each of the important sections gives directions about making new cells and other needed substances. These important sections determine the special traits of an organism. They are the genes.

Changing Plant Genes

7 By the beginning of this century, scientists had figured out, in general, what genes are and what they do. Using new tools and methods, they examined chromosomes to find individual genes. Through experiments, they discovered which genes did which jobs—for example, controlling how tall a plant will grow, or how much water it needs, or what color its fruit will be. They had even started to change the DNA they were studying.

---

[3] organism: any individual living animal or plant having parts that work together as a whole

American
VegetableGrower

Matthew Kramer
With 'Flavr Savr'

**Bright
Future For
Biotech
Vegetables**

**Can we use our knowledge of genes to
produce better vegetables? While many
warn of dangers, scientists and farmers
expect great improvements in food
production through research on genes.**

8   Researchers are able to cut a gene out of the
DNA from one living thing and put it into the
DNA from another organism. This is called *gene
splicing*. Let's say one kind of corn plant grows
tall and produces many ears of corn, but another
kind produces ears that taste better. Scientists can
take the height gene from the first plant and use
it to replace the height gene in the second plant.
The new corn plants will be taller, so they will
produce more of the better-tasting corn.

9   Some of the experiments have been quite strange. Scientists have put corn DNA into rice plants. They have put chicken DNA into potatoes. They have even put firefly DNA into tobacco plants. (The plants glowed in the dark!)

10   Scientists can also "turn off" a gene they don't want. This technique was used to produce the first "new" plant that made it to the grocery stores—a tomato called the Flavr Savr.

11   Most ripened tomatoes are too soft to truck them from one part of the country to another. Farmers pick them while they are still hard and green. Then the tomatoes are trucked to the stores or kept in cold storage for weeks. Just before they are sold, a gas is sprayed on them to make them turn red. This is why a grocery store tomato in the winter looks and tastes so different from one that ripens in the garden in the summer.

12   Scientists figured out which gene makes a tomato rot, and they changed the DNA around that gene to stop it from acting. With that gene turned off, the Flavr Savr tomato could stay fresh longer. It could be picked when it was riper and could keep

When scientists gathered in San Diego in 2001 to discuss gene experiments, so did protestors. This woman dressed as an ear of corn to get the attention of one of the scientists.

longer in the store. Unfortunately, high production costs killed the Flavr Savr.

13   A more important concern than improving taste is having food at all. With the population of Earth always growing, many people worry whether farmers can grow enough food for everyone. So one of the main goals of genetic study is to develop rice, corn, and other food plants that need less water and fertilizer but still produce large crops.

Changing Other Genes

14 Scientists aren't experimenting on just food. Some diseases are caused when a person's body does not make a substance it needs. The cause of the problem may be that a gene is not doing its job well. Scientists have found that they can trick tiny living things called bacteria into helping out. Bacteria are very simple, one-celled organisms. If human DNA is put into some bacteria, the bacteria can grow certain substances that humans need. This process is now used, for example, to create insulin,[4] needed by people with diabetes[5] [dī′ ə bē′ tēz].

15 Another cause of some diseases is genes that give incorrect directions. These diseases pass from parent to child. Maybe someday scientists will learn how to turn off or change these genes inside the parents. That way, their children will be born healthy.

16 "Wait a minute!" some people say. "Changing plants and animals? Is that a good idea? What if something goes wrong? What if the scientists make a new germ that can make us sick? And now they're working on humans? Where will all this lead?"

---

[4] insulin: a chemical that helps the body to process sugar and other foods

[5] diabetes: a disease in which, because of inadequate insulin, a person's cells cannot effectively process sugar and other substances

17 Some people are against changing the genes of any living things. They feel that this practice is working against nature and should not be allowed. For example, when the Flavr Savr tomato came out, demonstrators went to grocery stores to squash the new tomatoes.

18 Even more people are concerned about changing human genes. The practice may lead to more problems than it solves, they say. How can we foresee all the effects of even small changes? We may have to answer some very hard questions that we can't even imagine right now.

19 Can we afford to make changes in DNA? Can we afford not to? ◆

QUESTIONS

1. What does a chromosome look like?
2. How is a gene related to a chromosome?
3. What happens when scientists splice the genes of two different plants?
4. What is one way that changing some genes can help sick people?
5. Do you think scientists should change genes in living things? Why or why not?

AMERICA'S CITY

What lesser-known attractions lure visitors to our nation's capital city?

1　George Washington chose the site for the new nation's capital in 1791. At that time, this land hardly seemed like a good place for a capital. The land was marshy and bug-infested. People described it as a giant mud hole. And yet this area carved out of Maryland and Virginia would one day become the beautiful city of Washington, D.C. This year, millions of visitors from all over the world will come to Washington to take in the sights. The bustling, attractive city will not disappoint them.

2　When most Americans think of Washington, they picture the Capitol, the White House, and the Washington Monument. But D.C. offers other worthwhile attractions that are perhaps not as well known. If you are visiting Washington, why not check out some of these sights?

The Library of Congress is a major resource for our nation's lawmakers and for researchers. It is one of the many attractions in Washington, D.C., worth a visit.

81

The Library of Congress

3 What better place to check out than the Library of Congress? It is the largest library in the world. Opened in 1800 for use only by members of Congress, the library now is open to the public. It's hard to comprehend the size of its collection. It has more than 120 million items, including books, photographs, movies, and maps. When you get there, be sure to see the Main Reading Room. Look up at the great dome above you. Take a few moments to study the mosaics,[1] paintings, and statues that decorate the octagonal[2] room. Take a tour of the library. And don't miss the exhibit of the Gettysburg Address, handwritten by Abraham Lincoln himself.

National Archives

4 Every family needs a safe place to store its most important documents, such as birth certificates and deeds to the house. The place where the nation stores its documents is the National Archives [är´ kīvz]. Here you can see the treasured original copies of the Declaration of Independence, the Constitution, and the Bill of Rights.[3] Papers stored here include letters, maps,

---

[1] mosaic: a picture made with tiny bits of stone, glass, or tile
[2] octagonal: eight-sided
[3] Bill of Rights: the first 10 amendments, or additions, to the Constitution

People visiting the National Archives may view the original Declaration of Independence, which was drafted by President Thomas Jefferson in 1776.

diaries, photographs, and newspapers. In all, more than four billion pieces of paper are kept in this building. These precious documents are displayed inside bulletproof glass. Armed guards protect them during the day. Each night the documents are lowered into a bombproof vault.

Vietnam Veterans Memorial

5 In 1981 a contest was held to choose the design for a new memorial. The purpose of the memorial was to honor the Americans who

"The Wall" lists the names of all Americans killed or missing in the Vietnam War. Visitors seek out names of relatives and friends, and often leave gifts next to the wall.

fought and died in the Vietnam War.[4] Maya Ying Lin, a Chinese-American student, submitted a design. Her design suggested a monument unlike most other monuments, which often are statues made of stone. Instead, Lin proposed building a V-shaped wall of polished black granite.[5] The names of those killed in the war or missing in action would be etched on the wall. Visitors

---

[4] Vietnam War: a war fought in the Asian country of Vietnam from 1961 to 1975

[5] granite: a very hard rock that is used especially in building monuments

could walk along the wall, reading the names. The black wall filled with names would remind them of the sacrifice these soldiers made to the nation.

6   Although her design was unusual, Maya Ying Lin won the contest. "The Wall," as it is known, was built in 1982 and has become a favorite monument in D.C. Every day, it is visited by family members and friends of the fallen men and women. These visitors often leave letters, photographs, and personal items near the wall. They are joined by visitors of all ages from the United States and other parts of the world.

7   You may want to visit other parts of this memorial too. The Three Servicemen Statue, a bronze sculpture, stands near the wall. The nearby Vietnam Women's Memorial honors the more than 265,000 women who served in the war. The statue shows three servicewomen coming to the aid of a wounded soldier. Eight trees planted nearby are a reminder of the eight American nurses killed in Vietnam.

Korean War Veterans Memorial

8   A very different kind of memorial honors the veterans of the Korean War.[6] This memorial consists of 19 statues of soldiers. They are

---

[6] Korean War: a war fought in Korea from 1950 to 1953

The Korean War Veterans Memorial represents soldiers of each branch of the U.S. military: army, navy, marines, and air force.

dressed the way they would have dressed in the cold Korean winter. They seem to be making their way across a dangerous field. Looking into their faces, you can almost imagine what it felt like to be part of a group of soldiers far from home.

Museums for All Tastes

9   Washington, D.C., has some of the finest museums in the world. The respected Smithsonian Institution should be on your list of must-sees. The Smithsonian has 14 museums in Washington. Admission to all of them is free.

10   One of the Smithsonian museums is the National Air and Space Museum. This exciting

museum draws more than 10 million visitors each year. It may be the most visited museum in the world. Here you can see all kinds of exhibits on flying and space exploration. Don't miss the plane flown by the Wright brothers in 1903 and the command module[7] that carried U.S. astronauts to the Moon and back in 1969.

11   For a look at the country's past, visit the Museum of American History. There's something for everyone here. Some unusual items are on display, including George Washington's false teeth and Judy Garland's ruby slippers from *The Wizard of Oz*. Maybe you'll see Jackie Robinson's baseball glove and the huge flag that inspired our national anthem, "The Star-Spangled Banner." One of the museum's most popular exhibits is a collection of First Ladies' gowns.

Time Out for Fun

12   Washington is not just a place for memorials and museums. It is also home to nearly 600,000 people. If you visit D.C., you may want to take part in one of the city's special events. Just stroll around the Tidal Basin[8] during the Cherry Blossom Festival, which is held every spring.

---

[7] command module: a section that separated from a larger spacecraft, orbited the Moon, and returned to Earth

[8] Tidal Basin: a small lagoon in Washington, D.C., near the Jefferson Memorial

Gaze up at the beautiful pink and white blossoms on the cherry trees that the people of Japan gave to the United States. Also in the spring, be sure to catch the annual White House Easter Egg Roll. The Egg Roll is only for children age six or younger. Adults can't even enter the White House grounds that day unless they are with a child. But they can watch the kids search for the eggs and candy hidden all over the White House lawn.

13   Why not visit the city in the summer? You can be one of the nearly one million people who attend the Folklife Festival. The event has food, music, dance, and art from around the world. People from more than 50 nations and every part of the United States have joined in the fun.

14   And of course, on the Fourth of July in D.C., everyone is a Yankee Doodle Dandy. If you want to visit the city on Independence Day, you'd better plan ahead. All the hotels may be filled. Visitors pack the city on that special day. They come to see a parade, a concert, and a fireworks display.

15   The residents of Washington come from all parts of the world. One neighborhood celebrates its many cultures on Adams-Morgan Day in early September. That's when you can sample foods from Central America, Ethiopia, West Africa, the Caribbean, India, the Middle East, Vietnam, and more.

Anyone interested in flying machines should schedule an entire day at the National Air and Space Museum, part of the Smithsonian Institution.

Washington, D.C., has changed quite a bit since its swampy mud hole days. Visitors to the city will not see a marsh filled with bugs, but a vibrant town that is proud to be America's city.

QUESTIONS

1. Why is Washington, D.C., called America's city?
2. Name three Washington, D.C., attractions.
3. In what building can you see an original copy of the Declaration of Independence?
4. Describe the Vietnam Veterans Memorial. How is it different from most other memorials?
5. How many museums make up the Smithsonian Institution? Describe one of them.

PHOTO CREDITS